A. STO

ACPL ITEM
DISCARDED

3. 1833 00406 8570

Y0-ABH-904

250

CARVING

THE EASY WAY

CARVING THE TURKEY

Left — Removing leg, one prong of fork in drumstick, the other in second joint

Right — Dividing drumstick and second joint (small side platter)

Above—Removal of wing from body

Above — Long even slices of white breast meat

Left — Long - handled spoon for easy removal of dressing

Photographs, Courtesy Lewis & Conger

CARVING

The
EASY WAY

By

Lily Haxworth Wallace

M. BARROWS & COMPANY
INCORPORATED
Publishers   ·   New York

CIRCULATION DEPARTMENT

COPYRIGHT 1941 BY
LILY HAXWORTH WALLACE

Line Cuts Courtesy of
National Live Stock and Meat Board

First Printing, February, 1941
Second Printing, December, 1943
Third Printing, April, 1946
Fourth Printing, June, 1953

PRINTED IN THE UNITED STATES OF AMERICA
AMERICAN BOOK–STRATFORD PRESS, INC., NEW YORK

Contents

1125979

※ ※ ※

"Some hae meat and canna eat,
    And some would eat that want it;
But we hae meat, and we can eat,
    Sae let the Lord be thankit."
                    Robert Burns

※ ※ ※

※ ※ ※

When Father Carves the Duck.

"We all look on with anxious eyes
   When father carves the duck,
And mother almost always sighs
   When father carves the duck.
Then all of us prepare to rise
And hold our bibs before our eyes
And be prepared for some surprise
   When father carves the duck.

He braces up and grabs a fork
   Whene'er he carves a duck,
And won't allow a soul to talk
   Until he's carved the duck.
The fork is jabbed into the sides,
Across the breast the knife he slides,
And every careful person hides
   From flying chips of duck.

The platter always seems to slip
   When father carves a duck,
And how it makes the dishes skip,
   Potatoes fly amuck—
The squash and cabbage leap in space
We get some gravy on our face,
And father mutters Hindu grace
   Whene'er he carves a duck.

We thus have learned to walk around
   The dining-room, and pluck
From off the window-sills and walls
   Our share of father's duck;
While father growls and blows and jaws,
And swears the knife was full of flaws,
And mother jaws at him because
   He couldn't carve a duck."

Ernest V. Wright

※ ※ ※

Principles of Carving

THERE is no royal road to carving but with a general working knowledge of the anatomy of that which is to be carved almost any one may readily acquire skill. This assumes in the first place, that he or she has the proper tools to work with; practice in using them makes for perfection. Efficiency in carving depends almost equally on good tools and on the skill with which they are used.

Good carving is an accomplishment which adds much to the pleasure of the table. It is an essential adjunct to the well-served meal. Moreover good carving makes for economy, for he (or she) who skillfully wields the carving knife can unquestionably provide a greater number of attractive servings from a joint or a bird than one who is unskilled.

A good carver operates so deftly that every

portion served is sightly and palatable and does not contain a disproportionate amount of fat or bone. The working knowledge of the natural construction of various joints is indispensable to all who would attain proficiency and the best way to secure this knowledge is to make a study of meats before they are cooked, in order to acquaint oneself with the locations of bones and joints, of tough and tender muscles.

In carving any meat try as far as possible to cut it across the grain.

After the first incision has been made the angle at which the knife is held should never be changed. Each cut should be direct, sharp and incisive with long, clean, sweeping strokes to insure smooth, even slices—a sawlike motion inevitably results in jagged, uneven cutting. A good carver will make a joint go almost as far again as one who does not understand the art, yet with the good carver all will be well served.

Strength is not nearly as essential as neatness and care; a firm, steady hand and confidence in one's own ability will help materially. After a little experience you will easily distinguish between the choice and less choice portions.

Place meat on the plate attractively and with

the best side uppermost; even after all at the table have been served the meat remaining on the platter should not look jagged, rough or uneven but sufficiently inviting to tempt those who want a second serving.

Naturally where the whole of the joint may not be required at the first meal, neat carving means that the remainder is left in good shape for subsequent service.

One vital and all too often overlooked aid to easy carving is that the platter be large enough, not merely to hold the joint or bird as it stands, but to hold also the severed portions as they are cut. One sometimes sees platters so small or so overloaded with accompaniments and garnishes as to materially hamper the work of the carver. The persistency with which some housekeepers use a small platter, lest the meat look "lost" on a larger one, is a very sore point with many men.

The platter should be placed near enough to the carver that he may readily reach any part of the meat. Moreover, the cook should see to it that skewers and cords are removed before sending the meat to table, except in the instance of a rolled roast where a minimum amount of retained cord or skewering may be essential to hold the joint in shape.

Don't appear to make hard work of carving— that would seem to indicate that the joint or bird before you was not choice. Don't let yourself be hurried, though, on the other hand, work as rapidly as you can, especially with hot meat so that it may be served as hot as possible.

Where there is a choice, as between dark and light meat, inquire whether there is any preference on the part of a guest. (And, by the way, a word to that same guest—should your preference be asked and you have one, name it, always assuming that there is also enough for others who may prefer the same kind. But remember that with certain portions, the tenderloin for example in a steak, or the second joint in a bird, the preferred cuts are limited so be governed accordingly. One thing more, don't stare at the carver— you are invited to dine not to take a lesson in the art of carving and even though he may seem to be meeting with an occasional difficulty your role is to appear entirely unconscious of his efforts!)

Shall the carver sit or stand? Authorities differ, but let common sense be your guide. Admittedly if you can do equally good work seated, remain seated; on the other hand, there is no reason in the world why you should not stand if you want to, a small man or woman and a large joint should surely be permitted to meet on equal terms.

Finally, although this really has nothing to do with carving proper, "hot things hot and cold things cold" applies not only to the foods themselves but also to the serving platters and plates. A chilly plate cools off hot food placed upon it even faster than it takes to talk about it, while as for committing the gastronomic error of serving something cold on a lukewarm platter or plate—well there just isn't any punishment which adequately fits this crime!

Carving Equipment

Good carving cannot be accomplished unless the carver has good tools with which to work. Their number is few but their quality should be of the highest.

Standard Carving Set

The carving equipment of the average household consists of a standard "carving set," this comprising a knife with an eight or nine-inch semi-flexible blade, a two-pronged fork (with protective guard) and a steel. Such a set will serve for both roasts and poultry.

Steak and Small Poultry Set

A carving knife with five-and-a-half to six-inch stiff blade and matching fork for use with steaks, small roasts and birds. There is no steel with this set.

Poultry or Game Shears

Another very desirable adjunct to carving equipment is a pair of poultry or game shears which, with their strong handles and short, sturdy curved blades, separate joints and small bones better than a knife.

Carver's Helper (or Stabilizer)

A heavy, long wide-pronged fork sometimes used with large roasts or turkey to give greater control and hold them securely on the platter while being carved.

Over-size Carving Set

This comprises knife with nine to ten-inch semi-flexible blade and matching fork and steel and would be needed only for extra large roasts or large turkeys.

Slicer

This has a nine-and-a-half to ten-inch perfectly straight narrow flexible blade with rounded end and is used for slicing hams and large roasts. The shape of the blade permits a steady slicing motion without sawing and allows perfect control when approaching the bone.

Don't forget that while heretofore the terms "Sheffield," "Swedish" and "German" have been the only ones associated with fine cutlery steel, the United States now makes steel equal to, if not better in quality than most of the imported. Why should it not be so? We have the resources, we have the knowledge, and combined these make the best steel in the world.

Fish Carvers—A Silver (or Plated) "Slice" or Server with Matching Fork

The blade of the "slice" is broad and slightly curved upward, the fork proportionately broad and four-pronged.

A steel knife and fork should never be used for fish as contact with steel is apt to impair the fish flavor. This is especially true with certain choice varieties which owe their excellence largely to a characteristic individuality of flavor, and this might easily be destroyed or overpowered.

Lacking these, use any large silver or plated knife and fork (or spoon and fork) for serving.

Knives MUST be sharp—no one can carve satisfactorily with a dull knife and as a carving set is probably a once-in-a-lifetime investment it is economy to select the best possible quality so that the knife will take and hold an edge. Remember always that the blade is infinitely more important than the handle, so do not be led astray by beautiful handles which sometimes, though by no means always, are accompanied by poor steel.

Carving knives should be ground occasionally by an expert, and the steel of the set used in between times to true up the edge.

The use of the steel on the family carving knife should be in the kitchen and not at table, but of the two evils choose the lesser and if the carver cannot depend on kitchen cooperation or go to the kitchen himself to perform this rite by all means let it be done at the table, etiquette notwithstanding.

The Steel

The steel is used to true up the edge of the knife only, not to sharpen it. The knife must be sharp in the first place, the purpose of the steel is to KEEP it that way.

Technique of the Steel

Grasp firmly in the left hand with the thumb on top of the handle, the point of the steel being slightly away from the body. Taking the knife in the right hand place the heel of the blade (where it enters the handle) across the tip of the steel. Draw the blade down the steel lightly but steadily and always at the same angle along the

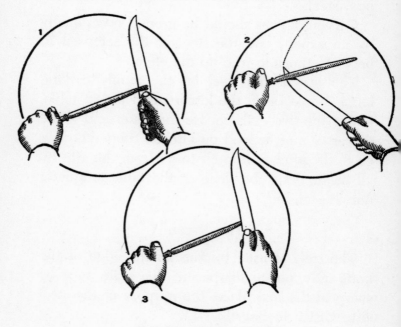

STEELING THE KNIFE

SHOWING THE PROPER POSITION OF HAND, KNIFE AND STEEL IN TRUING UP THE KNIFE IN PREPARATION FOR CARVING.

entire length of the blade, then pass the knife at the same angle against the under side of the steel and repeat original process. Use these alternate motions about a half dozen times on each side when you should have a good cutting edge.

It is not necessary to use any great weight or pressure in this operation, a firm steady even motion will do the trick.

If carefully done the entire length of the blade right from the tip to the heel will have been contacted by the time it has passed over the full length of the steel.

Knife Sharpeners

There are many excellent patent knife sharpeners on the market, some simple, some elaborate, some hand operated, others operated by electricity. Many have adjustable angle guides which make them adaptable to blades of varying thickness which necessarily require different angles for sharpening. Such sharpeners permit the amateur to obtain an even, correct angled edge along the entire length of the blade, and without scratching it.

CARE OF CUTLERY

All cutlery, but especially carving tools, should be kept and used for their legitimate purposes and for no other. Store the carving knife in its own appointed place away from other cutlery in order to keep the edge in perfect condition. If it came in an indented case, put it back into that case after using with its accompanying fork and steel.

We know one man who is so particular about his carving knife that he takes personal charge of it and puts it under his best shirts in his bureau drawer and then locks the drawer—but he's a fanatic on carving knives!

Carving Board for Kitchen or Pantry Carving

Where carving is done in the kitchen and this is the case in many homes, a carving board is a very useful piece of equipment. Boards made especially for this purpose are available but any firm one can be used. Try, though, to keep such a board for this use alone. Work expeditiously, arrange the carved portions of meat attractively on a hot platter, and, if possible, make all piping hot before bringing to table.

Carving at Table

Where carving is done by host or hostess at the table, place the meat platter directly in front of the carver and as near as possible to the serving plate. The carving knife, the tip of which may be on a knife rest of glass or silver, will be at the carver's right, the sharp edge turned inward, the fork (and steel if to be used) at the carver's left. In the best type of service only one serving plate will be in front of the carver the remaining ones at the left out of the way.

Sometimes, especially with a turkey, a small extra platter is placed at the left of the carver on which after its removal from the bird he can place the second joint and drumstick, thus making for easier division of the second joint among two or more guests. If this is done be sure that the extra platter is also piping hot.

Some silver meat platters are equipped with a fitted board and obviously this prevents scratching of the platter surface. Incidentally the board also makes for easier carving because its rougher texture prevents the meat from slipping.

What Shall Be Done with the Carving Knife and Fork after Using? There doesn't seem to be any hard and fast law on the subject. They may be laid together on the platter; they may even be placed one at each end of the platter; or they may be placed together with the tips on the knife rest. The main thing is that they shall not be put where they will drip either fat or gravy on the tablecloth.

Roast Beef:

"There is such a beautiful piece of beef in the larder; do somebody ask for a little slice of it."
Thackeray, "MEMORIALS OF GORMANDISING"

Steak:

"Bless the girls! a nice fresh steak was frizzling on the gridiron for our supper."
Thackeray, "THE FATAL BOOTS"

Tongue:

"Well that's a very good thing when it ain't a woman's."
Chas. Dickens, "PICKWICK PAPERS"

Corned Beef:

"What say you to a piece of beef and mustard? A dish that I do love."
Shakespeare, "TAMING OF THE SHREW"

"Sir" Loin of Beef:

"The sirloin of beef is said to owe its name to King Charles II of England, who, dining upon a loin of beef with which he was particularly pleased, inquired the name of the joint. Upon being told he declared its merit was so great that it deserved to be knighted, and that henceforth it should be known as Sir-Loin."

The Carving of Beef

THE first axiom to be laid down is that generally speaking all carving should be across the grain of the meat. The second, that roast beef is usually carved in thin slices though the personal preference of those being served will to some extent govern this. In any case each slice should be neat and attractive in appearance.

Standing Rib Roast

If the roast is heavy enough (two or three broad ribs) place it upright on the platter which it will touch only with the tip ends of the ribs and the section of back bone. This brings the browned fat on top; below this crisp fat is a thin strip of lean meat, which is not especially tender, and between this and the rib bones is the choice heart of the roast.

Place the roast on the table with the heavy

THE CARVING OF STANDING RIB ROAST

end to the left of the carver. If the joint has been properly prepared by the butcher, the end (back) bone will have been removed. If it has not been removed before cooking, the knife must be inserted between meat and bone, as close to the bone as possible, and the meat cleanly separated from the bone.

Insert fork (or carver's helper) firmly in the top of the meat, pressing it down through the flesh in order to hold the joint steadily in place. Beginning at the heavy end, carve thin slices from one end to the other, from left to right, cutting through the outer crispy fat, the less tender upper lean layer already referred to, and through the heart of the meat right down to the rib bone.

Carve as many slices as are desired, preferably before releasing the fork. It may be necessary after cutting several slices to turn the knife so that the blade is horizontal and, cutting parallel with the ribs, draw the knife along the bone to separate the cut slices from it.

Much of the fat is at the lower or thin end which in large roasts is frequently cut off and cooked separately as "short ribs" (often braised with vegetables) thus leaving only the choicest portion of the joint for roasting.

With a roast which is not broad enough (one, or sometimes even two, light ribs) to stand firmly upright, place it on its side on the platter, ribs toward the carver, then cut horizontal slices, loosening these from the bone, where necessary, by holding the knife vertically.

In this last instance the carver may wish to give the platter what might be called a half turn to the left rear as it stands before him, thus securing a better purchase on the meat and making his task a little easier.

Rolled Roast

This is exactly the same joint as the preceding one, with the single exception that the bones have been removed and the meat compactly tied and skewered into shape.

To carve, thrust the fork firmly into the meat, inserting it about half way through the joint on the left hand side; be sure that the guard of the fork is up. Then cut thin slices right across the surface of the meat, parallel with the platter.

Be careful to avoid the skewers with which the

THE CARVING OF ROLLED ROAST

[33]

meat has been fastened; these cannot be taken out before serving lest the roast fall apart, but as the carver comes to them, he will remove them, preferably by inserting the prong of a fork into the ring at the end of the skewer, if metal skewers are used. Wooden skewers must be removed either with the thumb and finger, or carefully "wiggled" out with the carving knife. If the roast is tied with cord instead of fastened with skewers, only one cord should be cut at a time, as it is reached.

Cut thin slices from right to left, lifting off each slice as it is cut.

Some carvers prefer placing a rolled roast fat surface uppermost, inserting the fork to the left, then carving down vertically from the top to the platter beginning at the right side of the roast.

It is always a graceful courtesy for the carver to inquire whether a guest prefers meat well done, medium, rare, or perhaps the crisp brown outside slice, for many people have a decided preference. With carefully roasted meat practically any taste may be catered to. Naturally the rarest slices will be found toward the center of the roast.

Roast Filet or Tenderloin

Insert fork in the roast at about the center in order to hold it firmly. Carve in even uniform slices approximately one-half inch thick, beginning at the heavier end which will be at the right of the carver.

POT ROASTS

1125979

Chuck or Blade Pot Roast

If possible remove bones (rib and blade) before bringing to table as this simplifies the carver's task. In this cut the fibers of the meat run in varying directions and on this account it is difficult, well nigh impossible, to carve in neat parallel slices as with a rib roast which is somewhat similar in general appearance. The following is perhaps the simplest method:

Separate the various contra-running muscles by running the tip of the knife around the connective tissue at the natural dividing lines. Take the first section thus divided and inserting the fork firmly into it give this portion of solid meat a half turn which will bring the grain of the flesh parallel with the platter. Slice down vertically across the grain in thin even slices one-fourth to

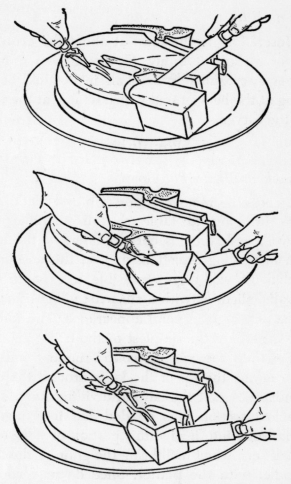

THE CARVING OF CHUCK OR BLOCK POT ROAST

one-third inch thick. Follow this same procedure with the remaining sections carving them in similar manner.

Rump Pot Roast

A solid pot roast from the rump, for example, is carved in similar manner to a filet or tenderloin, i.e. in slices right across the grain, but always thin, approximately one-fourth inch thick.

Rolled Pot Roast

Place with flattest side on platter, larger end to the right of the carver. Insert fork firmly into the meat toward upper left, then cut thin slices (one-fourth inch thick) beginning at the right, straight down through the roast, across the grain.

The strings cannot be removed until the carver reaches them as obviously they hold the roast in shape.

STEAKS

Contrary to generally accepted carving rules steaks are carved with the grain instead of across it, the reason being that the meat is tender and the fibers short.

It is always well in carving steaks to hold the knife at a slight angle; by this means the meat itself will be cut at an angle thus helping to retain the juices and prevent the meat drying out.

Carve a very thick steak into moderately thin slices; with a thin steak, on the other hand, they should be somewhat wider.

Porterhouse or T-Bone Steak

This steak has a bone running both across the end and down the center of the meat in the general shape of the letter T. Place on the platter so that the tenderloin is nearest the carver.

To carve, insert fork in meat, run tip of knife carefully alongside each bone (both sides of center bone) severing meat completely from it; then cut meat down (crosswise) into slices about three-fourths to one inch wide, serving a portion from below and a portion from above the bone to each guest.

If the bone is first entirely removed and placed at one side of the platter where it will not hinder the carver's work, the subsequent division of the steak will be very much simplified.

Quite frequently the thin flank or tail of the steak is cut off, trimmed of excess fat, ground and replaced. If a thin strip of the fat is left attached to the steak proper it can be drawn firmly

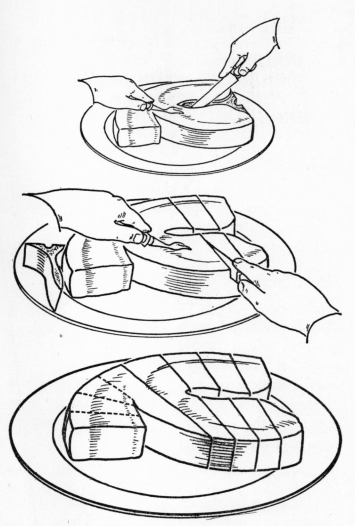

CARVING THE PORTERHOUSE STEAK

around this ground portion making a solid compact whole. Prepared in this way and broiled with the steak, the flank or tail is just as tender (though a little less choice) as the remainder of the steak.

Club Steak

The center bone of a club steak is small. This steak contains a fair portion of tenderloin and is of smaller size than porterhouse. Carve as porterhouse.

Sirloin Steak

A sirloin is a large juicy steak containing very little bone. What bone there is should first be removed when carving by cutting down close around it with the tip of the knife, after which, cut the steak across into inch wide slices; the size of these slices, however, will depend to some extent on the number of persons to be served from a given steak.

Filet Mignon

This is really the tenderloin of beef cut into slices from one to two inches thick. These, being broiled as individual steaks, need no carving.

Minute Steak

This may be sirloin or T-bone and consists of a very thin slice—so thin that it almost literally cooks "in a minute." This too, being an individual portion, needs no carving.

Planked Steak

Carve according to the directions given under the heading of whatever steak is being used and serve a portion of each vegetable or fruit accompaniment, with each portion of meat.

Any choice steak (approximately two inches thick) may be planked. In service this is the most elaborate of all steaks. The plank itself, usually of hickory, must be well seasoned before its first use by rubbing over with salad oil and heating slowly in the oven, repeating the process once or twice more if possible.

Note to Madame: Partially broil the steak before placing on the plank, then, having set it in position, surround it with a border of mashed potatoes, which will be more decorative if pressed through a pastry bag, after which complete the broiling of the steak during which time the potatoes will become tipped with brown. The remaining vegetable garnish-accompaniments are added just before serving, the plank itself being placed on a very large platter or oblong silver tray.

Fruit and vegetable garnish-accompaniments may be any two, three or more of the following: stuffed tomatoes or peppers, small mounds of peas, peas and carrots, string beans, asparagus tips, glazed onions or mushrooms, cauliflower flowerets, broccoli, carrot shreds, French fried onion rings, spinach timbales, grilled sweet potato slices, grilled pineapple slices, broiled bananas, broiled peach or apricot halves.

Round Steak

As a rule round steak is cut (by the butcher) somewhat thinner than porterhouse or sirloin. To carve cut across into slices about two inches wide.

Stuffed Flank (or Skirt) Steak

With either of these steaks the fibers are long but they may be artificially shortened by scoring crisscross fashion with a sharp knife part way through each steak. Because of the coarser texture and long fiber such steaks are best prepared by braising or slow moist cooking. A stuffed steak properly cooked is very good. Any preferred stuffing may be used, placing part of it on the already scored meat, then rolling up and tieing into shape.

To carve, cut into thin vertical slices from top to bottom right through the layers of meat and stuffing.

Tongue

Place tongue on the platter on its side, the larger end to the right of the carver, the rounded portion in front. Insert fork firmly in the meat and cut across into thin slices. The center of the tongue is the choice portion—about two center slices are allowed for each serving.

If the tip is used, it is best cut lengthwise, but with the root and trimmings, it may be reserved to be minced for sandwiches or made into potted tongue or used with various egg dishes.

CORNED BEEF

Brisket

This cut gives alternate layers of lean and fat meat. If possible remove bones before sending to table. Place the flat side down on the platter

[43]

with the larger end toward the right of the carver. With fork firmly inserted in the meat, cut down from the top to the bottom in thin slices, crosswise of the grain, beginning at the right.

Round or Rump

Cut from the top right down to the platter always across the grain of the meat. Both of these cuts consist almost entirely of lean meat with practically no fat.

"*Messenger was carving a loin of veal. Jem Messenger sat opposite him, eating bacon and beans on a very large scale.*"

Chas. Reade, "CLOUDS AND SUNSHINE"

"*Of course we must have something to eat . . . There'll be a cutlet—on a trunk—anyway.*"

Mrs. Humphry Ward, "LADY ROSE'S DAUGHTER"

"*A pair of boiled fowls, with tongue and* et ceteras, *were displayed at the top, and a fillet of veal at the bottom.*"

Chas. Dickens, "SKETCHES BY BOZ"

The Carving of Veal

Roast Loin of Veal

As WITH loin of pork opinions differ as to the best manner of placing this roast on the platter. It is a little easier to carve if the rib ends are up, the flat side resting on the platter, the meaty portion nearest the carver. Others prefer the exact reverse, maintaining that the meaty side is the more attractive and should therefore be placed away from the carver.

Insert fork firmly to the left of center and carve in vertical slices allowing one rib or chop to each service. If the kidney has been cooked with the loin serve as far as possible a small portion to each guest.

Note to Madame: See that the rib bones have been thoroughly severed where they join the back bone as instructed under Loin of Lamb and Loin of Pork.

Some like to bone a loin of veal, then to place the kidney in the cavity on the under side of the meat, roll the thin portion of the flank over it and tie compactly into approximately its original shape before roasting. If this is done the tieing cords must not be severed until the carver reaches each in turn.

Filet of Veal

Place on platter cut sides up and down. Insert fork at the left being sure the guard is up. If boned and stuffed carve right across the entire surface in horizontal slices about one-third inch thick, beginning at the right.

If the bone has been retained this will interfere with cutting right across the filet, so in this case slice horizontally as far as the small central bone, subsequently turning the meat around on the platter and proceeding in exactly the same manner with the second or left hand side of the filet as it was first placed on the platter.

Note to Madame: As the bone cavity is very small it is nice to prepare additional stuffing and cook it in a separate container. How about baking in muffin pans and using the little mounds as a garnish to the veal?

Roast Shoulder of Veal

This joint is almost invariably boned, stuffed and rolled, then tied in order to hold its form.

Place on the platter with the cut surface at right angles to it, insert the fork at about the center of the meat, then beginning at the right cut vertical slices right down through the meat and stuffing, removing the tieing cords as reached.

Veal Cutlet

There are two ways of serving Veal Cutlet. It may be cut into the thinnest of slices, placed between waxed paper on block and pounded to almost paper thinness, then dipped into egg and seasoned crumbs and sautéed. Having been cut into individual portions before being cooked no carving is necessary.

Sometimes, however, a cutlet is sautéed or braised whole, which means that it will be one to one-and-a-half inches thick. As the fibers run in various directions, easily distinguishable, it seems simplest to divide these according to their own contour. (See note under Chuck Pot Roast). Being short the fibers although running length-wise will still be tender.

Calf's Head

Calf's head although not very often seen on American tables is considered by many a great delicacy.

The head will have been split before cooking; the brains and tongue removed and cooked separately.

Place on the platter flat (bony) side down with the narrower (nose) portion toward the carver, then cut down from back to front in even slices one-fourth to one-third inch thick. The gelatinous portion around the eye is highly esteemed. After slicing the thick portion of the cheek down to the jawbone this bone may be slipped out and laid aside on the platter. The palate will then be exposed and a small portion of this with a little of the throat sweetbread served to each guest. The tongue, boiled and skinned, and a small portion of the brains should also be offered with each service.

Note to Madame: How is the head cooked? First soak for several hours in lukewarm water, changing the water from time to time, then very thoroughly cleanse and scrub. (We hope you have been able to persuade the butcher to remove the eyes—use ALL your powers of persuasion on him on this point!)

Now simmer the head gently until tender—about two hours. The favorite method of serving in England is to boil as directed, smother one half in a parsley sauce, sprinkle the second half generously with buttered crumbs and brown it in a moderately hot oven. Serve on separate platters, or both portions together on the one platter as you prefer.

"Mrs. Elton was growing impatient to name the day and settle with Mr. Weston as to cold lamb and pigeon pies."

Jane Austen, "EMMA"

"But a plain leg of mutton, my dear,
I beg thee get ready at three;
Have it smoking, and tender and juicy,
What better meat can there be?"
Thackeray, "MEMORIALS OF GORMANDISING"

"Dear Mrs. B: Chops and tomato sauce.
Yours, Pickwick"
Chas. Dickens, "PICKWICK PAPERS"

The Carving of Lamb

Roast Leg of Lamb

A LEG of lamb has a straight rod-like bone running directly through the leg, somewhat off center, the meat being heavier on one side of the bone than on the other. Frequently two or three chops are left on at the heavy end of the leg.

Place meat before the carver with the heavier side of the meat uppermost on the platter, or, in other words, away from the carver. This means that with a left leg the protruding slender bone will be at the carver's right; with a right leg the position will be reversed. Some insist that the shank end should always be at the left of the carver, but especially in view of the fact that the best slices come from the heavier meaty section, known as the cushion and that it is easier to carve when that cushion is at the far side of the platter, surely the comfort of the carver should take precedence over the position of the meat on the platter itself.

To carve, insert the fork firmly in the meat at the left, then beginning near the center, cut several vertical slices from the outer (rear) surface through the heavy side of the meat right down to the bone, after which turn the blade of the knife and slip it under the cut slices, parallel with the bone, to separate the cut meat from it. This gives correct cuts of meat across the grain.

Another method often used is to start slicing at the thick end of the joint, cutting off the chops first, then continuing to slice the meat as above from the outer surface down to the bone. If necessary, with many to be served, turn the joint over and cut similarly from the thinner side, also down to the bone. Some consider the knuckle muscle (a small rather glutinous morsel found at the shank end) a choice bit.

The protruding shank bone of a leg of lamb may be decorated with a paper frill, similar to, but larger than a cutlet frill, cut with scissors from a folded strip of not too heavy white paper. The French have a name for this—they call it a

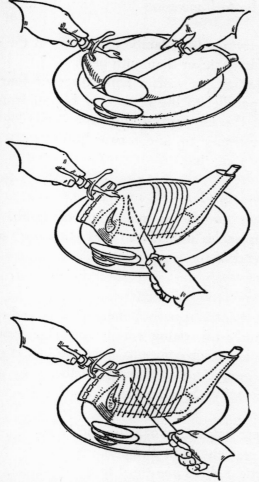

THE CARVING OF ROAST LEG OF LAMB

"Manchette," meaning literally a little cuff or ruffle.

In carving either lamb or mutton cut the slices somewhat thicker than with beef.

If desired, as with a ham, three or four thin slices parallel to the bone may be cut from the side of the leg nearest the carver, the leg then slightly tipped up and forward on the platter to facilitate carving.

Boiled Leg of Lamb

Carve exactly as roast leg of lamb. Here though one is unlikely to find chops left at the thick end of the leg.

Roast Stuffed Shoulder of Lamb

This joint is usually boned, stuffed and rolled. Obviously the tieing cords cannot be removed until the carver comes to each one in the course of his operations as if removed the meat would, of necessity, break apart and the stuffing be exposed.

Insert fork to left of roast and beginning at the right end cut right through from top to bottom in vertical slices one-third to one-half inch thick.

Occasionally a shoulder of lamb is plain roasted

without boning and stuffing. Owing to the formation of the bone it is a somewhat difficult piece of meat to carve as the fibers run in varying directions and it is not easy to get nice even slices.

This particular joint is one not very often seen but the meat is tender and flavorful though somewhat fatter than the leg. If desired the shank bone may be decorated with a paper frill; see Roast Leg of Lamb.

Mock Duck

A boned shoulder of lamb is the cut generally used to make "Mock Duck," a sage and onion forcemeat replacing the bone, the shank of which is inserted at one end for the duck's "bill," the flat blade bone being put at the other end of the roast to masquerade as his "tail."

Carve as stuffed shoulder of lamb.

Crown Roast of Lamb

This is quite the easiest of all joints to carve, it only being necessary to cut down between each two ribs, allowing one chop, or with very young consequently small meat, two for each service.

Note to Madame: A crown roast is usually prepared by the butcher and consists of two groups of ribs with the end or chine bones removed, the chops Frenched and trimmed of excess fat, after which the two sections are firmly fastened together with cord in the shape of a crown, meat sides in. Trimmings from the meat may be passed through the food chopper, seasoned and pressed into the center cavity or a bread stuffing may take the place of the meat; again, if preferred, roast plain without any stuffing at all. It is well to force a piece of fat pork over each protruding bone to prevent scorching. When serving, remove the pork and replace with paper cutlet frills or impale a large stuffed olive on each bone.

Roast Loin of Lamb

A loin of lamb (or mutton) consists of several loin chops roasted together instead of being separated and broiled. Great care must be taken to sever the chop bones thoroughly before cooking in order to facilitate carving. If the chine (back) bone is completely removed before cooking the carver's task will be greatly simplified.

Insert fork to left and beginning at the right

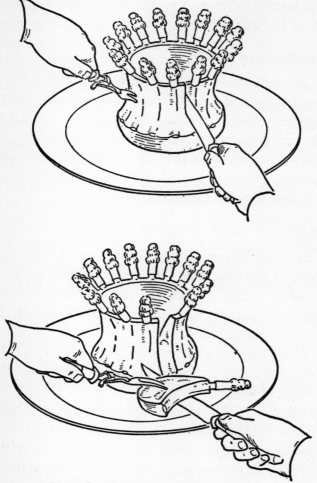

THE CARVING OF CROWN ROAST

cut vertically from top to platter allowing one chop to each service.

Rib Roast of Lamb

This is a grand small roast for "Him and Her," consisting of the portion usually served as chops roasted whole. Exert the same care in regard to chopping through the bone or removing the chine bone as with the loin in order to simplify carving.

Carve exactly as loin of lamb.

Saddle of Lamb or Mutton

A "saddle" consists of the two unseparated sides of the loin. The thin under portion or flank is rolled under the heavier part of the meat and this operation is made easier if the rib bones are first cut rather short.

Place on the platter with the tail end to the left of the carver. Insert the fork firmly near the center, and carve down to the ribs in long slices, parallel with the back bone and the whole length of the saddle, then slip the knife under and separate the slices from the ribs. Do exactly the same on the other side of the back bone. Divide the slices if very long.

Turn the meat over on the platter, cut out the choice tenderloin and serve a little of this with a small portion also of the crisp flank fat to each guest.

Admittedly carving a saddle of lamb or mutton in this way is cutting with the grain of the meat, but it is the mode adopted by the best authorities, and only the finest quality meat, very tender due to long hanging, will be used here.

Forequarter of Lamb

A forequarter of lamb consists of practically half of one side of a lamb, comprising the shoulder, breast and rib chops. It is rather difficult to carve; the shoulder must first be separated from the lower bony portion, this being done by inserting the fork into the shoulder section then running the tip of the knife around the shoulder and, holding this firmly with the fork, continue the cutting, so as to separate the two portions. A slight backward, upward pressure exerted on the fork helps to separate the two with very little incision of the knife, except on the outer surface. A second hot platter should be provided on which to lay the shoulder while carving the remainder of the forequarter.

Unless the bones of the chops have been carefully severed at the thick end before cooking, it will be almost impossible to divide them. The rib bones too must be cleanly cut across at about the center before cooking, as otherwise the bones would be too long and ungainly to handle gracefully.

Serve a chop and a small portion of the shoulder to each.

Only young spring lamb would be served as a forequarter.

"For the first course at the top, a pig, and pruin sauce."

Goldsmith, "SHE STOOPS TO CONQUER"

"One would not, like Lear, 'give anything.' I make my stand upon pig."

Chas. Lamb

"I wish you could ha' seen the shepherd walkin' into the ham and muffins."

Chas. Dickens, "PICKWICK PAPERS"

The Carving of Pork

Roast Loin of Pork

THIS may consist of part or all of the loin and the tenderloin may or may not be removed. The rib bones must be thoroughly severed from each other at the heavy (back bone) end before cooking to expedite carving and, if the butcher has been instructed to remove the back or chine bone itself, this too will be found of the utmost help.

Opinions differ as to the best manner of placing this roast on the platter. Some prefer the rib ends up with the meat side nearest the carver. Others exactly reverse this, holding that if the bony side is placed nearest the carver the guests see the more attractive part of the meat.

Insert the fork at the left in the heavy part of the meat between the ribs, and beginning at the right, cut down between each two rib bones, allowing one rib or chop to each service. With very heavy meat, or if thinner slices are desired, cut one portion with a bone, the next without, by making the first cut as close as possible to the left side of the first rib, the second close to the right side of the second rib, and so on.

If desired the rib bones of the roast may be decorated with small paper frills.

Boned Loin of Pork

Some like to bone a loin of pork then to roll the thin end over and tie the meat compactly into approximately its original shape before roasting. In this case carve down into medium thin vertical slices beginning at the right end of the roast, severing each tieing cord as it is reached.

Crown Roast of Pork

Carve and serve exactly as directed for crown roast of lamb.

HAM

Baked Whole, Fresh or Smoked

Here again as with a leg of lamb one must remember that there will be a right and a left

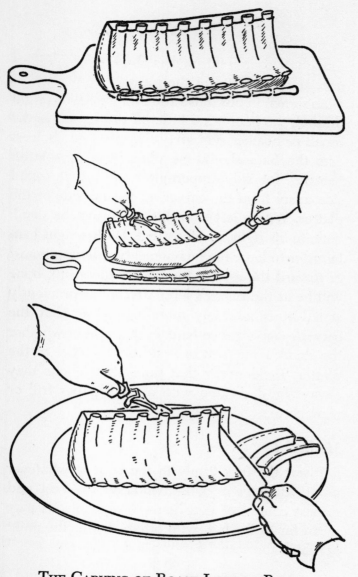

THE CARVING OF ROAST LOIN OF PORK

though of course this makes absolutely no difference to the quality of the meat.

As shown in our illustration the bone runs right through the ham but a little off center and as the broad or heavier side gives the best and choicest cuts the ham should be placed on the platter (always fat side uppermost) with that broad side away from the carver, at the far side of the platter. With a left ham this will bring the shank bone to his right, as illustrated. With a right ham in order to have the heavy meaty side uppermost or toward the rear of the platter the shank bone will be at the carver's left. After all as previously stated it is infinitely more important that the carver's convenience be considered than whether the shank bone is at one end or the other of the platter. Incidentally that same shank bone may always be decorated with a small paper frill or manchette.

Method I

Insert the fork firmly in the ham at whatever point will give you, individually, the best and firmest control of that ham—with some this may mean far to the left, with others nearer the point at which the actual carving is done.

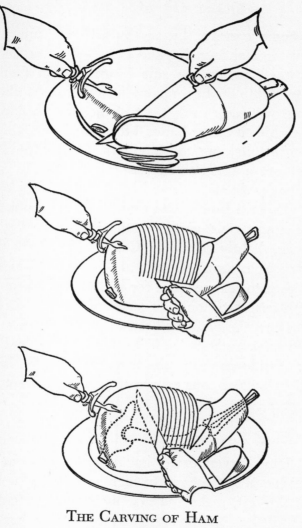

THE CARVING OF HAM

Some carvers like, in the very beginning, to cut three or four thin slices parallel to the length of the ham on the side nearest them, then to slightly tip the ham up and forward on the platter so that it rests on that cut surface thus making it possible to carve better broader slices.

Now, holding the ham firmly with the fork, cut out a small thick (or wedge shaped) slice near the shank bone and lay it aside. Then carve right down from the top surface to the bone and at almost right angles to that bone holding the knife slightly slantwise. Cut several slices, then if necessary run the knife along the bone parallel with it to release these for service. A little of the rich crisp fat should be served with each slice.

When the ham has been carved right across to the thick end, it should be turned over and the other side carved in the same manner—the lower slices will of course be a little smaller than the first ones.

Method II

Some carvers prefer beginning to carve at the thick end of the ham. In such case insert the fork at the left, make the first incision just right or left of the aitch-bone depending on whether one is carving a left or a right ham, and work right across from the thick end toward the narrower shank end.

Baked Half Ham, Smoked

A half ham is easier to carve than a whole one. With it one invariably begins to work at the already cut side. As with a whole ham place on the platter fat side uppermost. Hold firmly in position by inserting the fork deeply into the fleshy part at about the center top, then slice down in thin even vertical slices, this applying equally whether the shank or the butt end has been selected.

Baked Smithfield Ham

Smithfield Ham is different from ordinary ham, possessing a rich, rare quality which has made it famous the world over. You cannot eat as much of this ham as you can other meat. It is richer than almost any other food. A few thin slices of this delicious red meat and you have enough for one sitting.

To carve start on the back, about two inches from the end of the hock bone, letting the first cut be straight down to the bone. Then gradually slant the knife and cut out a number of good sized slices, after which you can cut off thin slices, about one-eighth of an inch thick. In cutting, a sharp knife should be used and should be held at an angle of about forty degrees.

Note to Madame: Here is an interesting old Virginia recipe * for the cooking of Smithfield Hams:

Lay your ham in cold water and, after allowing it to soak for half an hour, scrape and wash it thoroughly. When it is absolutely clean, put it to soak in fresh water and leave it from twelve to thirty-six hours, according to its age and size. Then take a large pot with plenty of water, put in your ham (skin down) with onions, a little celery, some parsley, two or three blades of mace, and half a dozen cloves. (Any of these garnishments may be omitted, according to your individual taste.) Put the pot on the fire, and as it comes to a boil, skim it well. Then allow it to simmer until it turns over of its own accord in the pot.

When the ham has "done turn over," as the colored folks say, which is caused by the gradual swelling of the fat changing its center of gravity,

* Courtesy Pender's Department Grocery, Norfolk, Virginia.

[74]

set it off the fire to cool in its own water. Do not let it get cold, but as soon as it is cool enough to handle place it upon a wooden board and, using a clean cloth, pull off the skin.

Then on the glistening expanse of fat sprinkle a good covering of white pepper. A quarter of a pound is not too much to use on a big ham. Then stud it with finest cloves, pressing them into the fat about an inch apart. Next, take plenty of "open kettle" sugar, the light brown sugar that grandmother used, and put as thick a layer as possible on top of the peppered ham. You can get a sugar coating more than an inch thick, if you work expertly.

Then place the ham in an iron pan into which you have poured a pint of good sherry or an equal quantity of fine cider. Put it in a very slow oven, and little by little the sugar will melt through the fat, carrying the pepper and the taste of cloves right through to the bone.

Some of the sugar may run down the sides of your ham into the sherry or cider with some of the fat, but if your oven is not too hot at least four-fifths of the sugar will sink into the ham itself. Towards the end of the cooking, baste the ham with the sherry or cider, and drippings, and it finally comes out a rich, dark brown, studded with the "coffin nails of Asia," as cloves were called after the Portuguese had ravished its rich coasts in search of this most fragrant of all spices. There is nothing finer in the world than a slice of this cold ham.

Stuffed Shoulder of Pork, Fresh

With a boned stuffed shoulder of pork the problems of carving are greatly simplified there being no bone to interfere with the carving knife. Carving begins preferably at the heavy end of the meat, the slices being cut vertically from the top right down to the platter through the upper side of the meat, the stuffing and the lower side of the meat.

Because the bone cavity is small, therefore cannot hold very much stuffing, more may be prepared and cooked separately, see Filet of Veal. (Page 48)

Pork Tenderloin

The fibers in a tenderloin of pork, as in a tenderloin of beef, run lengthwise.

Fresh pork tenderloins unfortunately are usually split lengthwise before sautéing or broiling. We say "unfortunately" because by this means due to those long fibers, they may be anything but "tender." If prepared in this way there is nothing to do but serve them as they are. A better method, however, is to French them, i.e. have them cut by the butcher into one or one and a half inch crosswise slices which are then flattened by pounding, resulting in delicious tender short-fibered meat needing no carving but served as individual portions.

Stuffed Pork Tenderloins

Where pork tenderloins are stuffed, rolled, tied and baked, divide for service into halves or thirds according to their size, by slicing vertically (across the fiber) as they lie on the platter.

Fresh Spareribs, Roast or Broiled

Fresh spareribs are the flat rib bones which have been cut away from the side meat before it is cured for bacon. They are delicious and appetizing, succulent and savory but without very much meat. The bones are chopped across by the butcher and for serving are cut into medium sized portions allowing three or four of the rib bones to each.

Corned Spareribs

Corned spareribs as usually cooked and served with sauerkraut, are cut into pieces convenient for serving before cooking, thus needing no carving.

Roast Suckling Pig

Place on the platter so that the head is to the left of the carver. First sever the head at the neck, the bones of so young an animal being very tender, carving is not difficult. Next, take off the shoulders and hams by cutting through the crisp skin and the meat with a circular motion from the lowest forward point around and up almost to the back bone, thence down to the platter again. With the fork firmly imbedded in each partially severed joint bend it backward from the base and cut through at the knuckle.

Insert fork at left of body near neck, make a sweeping cut right down the body from neck to tail and finally divide into portions cutting from the back bone through the ribs vertically, first on the near side, then on the further one.

Serve a portion of the rib meat and a portion of leg or shoulder meat to each with a little of the cheek as far as it goes.

THE CARVING OF PORK

Note to Madame: Only a very small pig is roasted whole. It may be stuffed with a chestnut, onion or bread stuffing or left unstuffed. If the former, skewer the meat together over the stuffing and truss with the forelegs resting forward, the hind legs backward that it may lie flat for service.

Turkey:

"The turkey is beyond doubt one of the finest presents the New World has made the Old."

Brillat-Savarin

Chicken:

"She sat down in solitude to cold tea and the drum sticks of the chicken."

Mrs. Gaskell, "WIVES AND DAUGHTERS"

Goose:

"At last the dishes were set on and grace was said. It was succeeded by a breathless pause as Mrs. Cratchit looking all along the carving knife, prepared to plunge it in the breast of the goose; but when she did, and when the long expected gush of stuffing issued forth, one murmur of delight arose all round the board."

Chas. Dickens, "CHRISTMAS CAROL"

Duck:

"That I may reach that happy time
The kindly gods I pray,
For are not ducks and peas in prime
Upon the last of May?"

Thackeray, "POEMS"

The Carving of Poultry

PERHAPS the simplest way of all to learn to carve a chicken is to disjoint it in preparation for a stew or fricassee, for it is then possible to study the anatomy of the bird; to work the leg and wing bones back and forth in their sockets and thus discover where the joints are located. Lacking an opportunity of studying the structure of a bird in this way, practice and practice alone, of course plus the use of correct carving equipment, will make a good poultry carver.

Assuming though that one has an opportunity of practicing on an uncooked bird this is the method to follow:

After the chicken has been singed, drawn, washed inside and out, patted dry with a cloth, the oil bag removed from the top of the tail and the neck cut off and laid aside with liver, gizzard and heart for subsequent use in making gravy, place the bird in front of you, breast up and wings toward the left. With a small sharp knife cut through the thin, probably rather loose skin between the insides of the legs and the body, then bend the legs over toward you and you will readily see not only where the joint is because the leg bone moves in its socket but also where the heavy flesh joins the body.

Now make a clean cut through the flesh on either side of the bone, then, still bending the leg downward toward you, cut through right at the joint itself without breaking or splintering the bone. Continue to cut right down through the lower flesh and skin thus severing the leg completely from the body of the bird. It is now easy to divide the leg, again absolutely at the joint, separating the drumstick from the thigh or second joint.

Now cut through the skin above the wing, working that wing back and forth until you have discovered where the joint is which attaches wing to body and, as with the leg, bend the wing toward you, cut through the flesh of the shoulder down to the joint, at which point it will be severed from the body by cutting through the lower connecting skin.

Turn the bird around and proceed in the same manner with the second leg and wing.

The "wish bone" may now be cut off with its adhering meat. To do this make an even slanting cut from the front of the breast bone down to the shoulder on either side, then cut through the cartilage between the tip of the collar bone and the breast. For a fricassee, breast and back bones will probably be cleanly cut through with a knife, so for the moment let us end our anatomy lecture here and proceed to table—but please examine the breast structure for later carving of white meat.

It must not be assumed that this kitchen practice alone will make an expert carver. It does, however, give the tyro an opportunity of learning more easily than can be done after a bird is cooked, just where the joints come and how they can be cleanly and smoothly separated.

Roast Chicken or Turkey

The general bone structure of turkey and chicken are so similar that directions for carving one really govern both.

Place the bird on its back on the platter, drumsticks toward the right. Insert carving fork firmly into the leg, one prong through the drumstick, the other through the second joint. Cut around the second (thigh) joint and, pressing against the body of the bird with the flat part of the blade of the knife and using the fork more or less as a lever, draw the leg toward you from the body. If necessary use the knife to separate the leg right at the thigh joint cutting through the flesh and skin on the under side of the leg.

If a separate smaller platter or a plate has been provided, as in the instance of a turkey, lift the entire leg (second joint and drumstick) to that platter, laying it skin side down because the inner (cut) surface permits the joint to be more clearly seen and therefore more easily divided. Next, cut right at the dividing joint into two portions, from which it will subsequently be easy to cut lengthwise slices for service. The second joint is the choice part of the dark meat and each second joint of a turkey may be divided to give two or more portions. With a small or medium-sized chicken usually the second joint makes one service only and no side plate would be provided.

Now remove the wing at the joint, using the fork as a lever as before, pressing against the body of the bird with the knife. Please note here that the wing joint is closer to the body than the thigh joint is to the back bone.

Insert fork firmly and deeply across the breast bone and beginning at the left carve long even slices of white meat from the breast. Under the back, attached to each side of the back bone, will be found a small solid piece of dark meat, tender and delicious, known as the "oyster." The "parson's" or "pope's" nose (the tail tip), a favorite tidbit, is easily severed with the point of the carving knife.

The drumsticks, especially of a turkey, are usually trimmed with paper frills, these having been originally designed for the benefit of the carver so that he might take hold of the drumstick and give it a twist to help sever it from the body after making the first incision with the carving knife. With a very tender bird and a sharp knife, finger handling may not be necessary though there is no law against it if it really helps the individual carver.

If the tendons have been drawn, as they should be before cooking, the drumstick is by no means to be despised; alternatively, if the feet have been cut off without drawing the tendons, this particular joint will necessarily be more difficult to manipulate.

In bygone days, the liver of a chicken was usually impaled on the skewer which fastened the wings in trussing and was supposed to add richness to the wing it touched, which was referred to as "the liver wing" and was looked upon as the choicer of the two.

If the entire bird is likely to be used, both legs and wings may be removed before beginning to carve the breast although usually the practice is to carve all the meat (dark and light) from one side before carving the opposite side. With a small family probably but one-half of the bird will be needed at one meal.

Serve a spoonful of dressing with each portion of meat.

Note to Madame: Be very careful to see that all trussing pins, skewers and cords are removed before sending the bird to table lest you invoke the wrath of the carver.

Roast Capon

Follow directions for carving roast chicken. The legs will be a little larger, the breast fuller and plumper and this last will therefore give more slices of white meat than the average chicken.

Roast Goose or Duck

While delicious in flavor the meat is scant in quantity as compared with the bone. Place before the carver with the wing end to the left. Insert the fork firmly with one prong on each side of the very slight ridge of the breast bone and beginning at the left, work from the outside (nearest to carver) toward the center, and holding the knife with the blade slightly slanted outward, cut thin parallel slices the entire length of the breast, until the ridge bone is reached. Now slip the knife under the meat as close to the bone as possible to sever the meat from the carcass. Carve the second side of the breast in the same manner and, only if necessary, serve the wings.

To separate the legs from the body, it will be found desirable to tip the bird over very slightly on the platter by means of the fork, for the thigh joint lies nearer the back bone than with turkey or chicken. It furnishes more resistance and is more difficult to carve. Both leg and wing may, if preferred, be severed before carving the breast slices.

There is no white meat on either goose or duck, even the choice breast meat being dark. Remember always that the leg of a flying bird and the wing of a swimmer are the choicer portions, because in swimming the bird uses (and consequently toughens) the leg muscles, a similar action taking place in the wings of a flying bird.

Note to Madame: The tougher leg and wing portions with what little meat may be found on the back of a duck provide a savory second service as ragout or salmi.

Pigeon and Squab

The difference in these birds is solely that of name and age, a squab being a young (approximately four weeks old) pigeon. Squab, being small, are usually served whole, one to a person. Pigeons, being somewhat larger, are at times split, in which case cut right down through the center. Either bird may be roasted whole or split open and broiled.

Note to Madame: Pigeons too old to roast make excellent pigeon pie if simmered gently in water or stock until tender, well seasoned, topped with pie crust and baked.

Broilers—Chicken, Duckling, Turkey Poult

All broilers will have been prepared by splitting down the back then removing the back bone before cooking that they may lie flat on broiler or grill. Sometimes they are actually divided lengthwise before cooking in which case no subsequent carving is needed. If this has not been done they may be divided at table by cutting into lengthwise halves right down through the breast, allowing half a bird (breast, leg and wing) to each portion. Larger birds may be deftly quartered lengthwise and crosswise with poultry carvers or poultry shears.

In any case they will be placed on the platter with the inner or bony side nearest the platter and the crisp browned flesh side uppermost.

Wild Fowl:

"*A dish of wild fowl, that came afterward, furnished conversation for the rest of the dinner.*"
Addison, "Sir Roger de Coverley"

For the more genteel, snipe, woodcock, partridge, pheasant, quail, we'll serve."
W. Cartwright, "The Ordinary"

"*Hares, pheasants, partridges, snipes, barndoor chickens (those tame villatic fowl) capons, plovers . . . I dispense as freely as I receive them.*"
Chas. Lamb, "Essays of Elia"

Venison:

"*The dinner was as well-dressed as any I ever saw. The venison was roasted to a turn—and everybody said they never saw so fat a haunch.*"
Jane Austen, "Pride and Prejudice"

"*Those unctuous morsels of deer's flesh were not made to be received with such dispassionate services. I hate a man who swallows it, affecting not to know what he is eating.*"
Chas. Lamb

The Carving of Game and Venison

Roast Rabbit, Hare or Squirrel

Place on the platter back uppermost, fore legs toward the left. To carve, separate both fore and hind legs at the second joint, cutting around these in the same manner as suggested for the carving of a suckling pig. Divide the back crosswise into three portions, or carve in slices as with saddle of lamb or mutton, i.e. parallel with the back bone.

The choicest portions and, in fact, the only ones suited to service as a roast are the saddle and second joints.

Note to Madame: In trussing, turn the fore legs backward and the back legs forward, skewering and tieing them firmly into place. Either may be stuffed or roasted plain. The meat is dry, for which reason constant basting is necessary during the cooking process which should preferably be done in a double roaster. Larding or barding too helps to make the meat richer and moister.

(Larding = drawing very narrow strips of fat salt pork through the meat with a larding needle made for the purpose. Barding = enveloping in or covering with a blanket of thin slices of fat salt pork or bacon.)

Fried or Broiled Rabbit, Hare or Squirrel

Here again the back and second joints will be the only parts so served. They will have been divided into individual portions before cooking, therefore need no carving at table.

Roast Wild Duck

Usually only the breast is served. Carve by making a lengthwise cut down the center of the breast after which turn the blade of the knife, slip it under the meat and remove each half of the breast from the carcass in one thick slice.

The gourmet then puts the carcass into a press and uses the juice thus extracted as gravy or sauce for the breast. The legs make an excellent salmi by gently cooking with added seasonings and wine.

Broiled Wild Duck

Mallard ducks are split down the back and broiled as domestic ducks; Teal are usually left whole. If large enough divide the breast into two portions for service, running the knife lengthwise down the center of the breast, turning the blade and removing each half of the breast meat in one slice as with roast wild duck.

Roast Partridge or Pheasant

Place on platter with wings to the left. With larger birds cut through the meat from above the joint of the wing down along the leg, thus removing both leg and wing together. Slip the knife under the breast meat, close to the bone, remove each half of the breast entire, then divide it crosswise through the center to make two portions of each side.

If the birds are small serve half to a portion.

A Word about the Service of Small Birds— Grouse, Quail, Woodcock, Snipe

Being small birds, served whole, no carving is necessary—they are all individually prepared, individually served. Any may be carefully broiled or roasted.

Note to Madame: Woodcock are usually not drawn, epicures considering the entrails a delicacy. For those, however, who do not care for them remember that these same entrails shrivel during the cooking and may easily be discarded.

Any of the above birds should be barded or very thoroughly basted while cooking.

Venison

Roast Leg of Venison

Carve exactly as directed for leg of lamb, cutting vertical slices of moderate thickness, beginning at the heavier part of the leg and cutting right down to the central bone, finally running the blade of the knife under the meat parallel to the bone to separate the slices.

Saddle of Venison

Carve exactly as directed for saddle of lamb or mutton, remembering that venison fat very quickly chills and hardens, for which reason speed is essential and both mutton and venison must be served on thoroughly heated platters and plates.

Haunch of Venison

This corresponds to a hind quarter of lamb, consisting therefore of leg and loin.

Place on the platter with the loin or back bone nearest the carver. Separate the leg from the loin (if the rump and aitch bones have been taken out when the deer was divided the carver's work will be greatly simplified) and carve the loin by cutting down between the ribs into individual chops; or, if preferred, the meat may be cut into slices parallel with the back bone as in the instance of a saddle.

Carve the leg exactly as a leg of lamb and serve a portion of leg and a portion of loin meat to each.

"*Three days out of the seven, indeed, both man and master dined on nothing else but the vegetables in the garden, and the fishes in the neighboring rill.*"

Bulwer, "My Novel"

Salmon:

"*Next came a great piece of salmon, likewise on a silver dish.*"
Thackeray, "The History of Samuel Titmarsh"

"*A little piece of salmon, cut out of the fish's centre.*"
Chas. Reade, "It Is Never Too Late to Mend"

Cod:

"*Said he upon this dainty cod,
how bravely I shall sup.*"

Thomas Hood, "Poems"

The Carving and Serving of Fish

As ALREADY stated a broad silver or plated slice or server with its accompanying fork is best adapted to the attractive service of fish. Failing these, however, a silver spoon and broad fork or silver knife and fork must be substituted.

As little of the bone as possible should be served with any fish which must be divided carefully in order not to break the delicate flakes.

Planked Fish

Planked fish are almost invariably split before cooking, the center bone may or may not have been removed, if retained it keeps the fish in firmer and better shape; if removed, however, it simplifies the work of the carver.

To serve cut lengthwise through the center, then across into convenient pieces for serving. The center cuts are the choice ones. Serve a portion of each accompanying vegetable garnish, peas, tomatoes, Duchesse potatoes, etc., with each helping.

Stuffed Baked Fish

Place on platter with head to the carver's left. Cut through the skin parallel with the back bone from head to tail of the fish, then cut down vertically into portions first the front, then the rear side, serving a little stuffing with each helping and leaving the back bone intact on the platter.

Some find it easier to serve the front side of the fish, then to detach and lay the center bone aside before serving the rear half of the fish.

Note to Madame: A stuffed fish is usually cooked in upright position, i.e., the stuffing sewed into place in the stomach cavity, the fish then skewered in slightly rounded or curved position, back uppermost, head and tail being left on. Remove skewers and strings before serving.

Broiled Fish

The larger broiled fish (mackerel or bluefish) are split open before cooking. For serving they must be divided lengthwise down the center, each half then divided again into individual por-

[104]

tions, the center cuts as always being the most desirable.

Small fish, broiled, or fried, also filets, are served as individual portions, thus requiring no carving.

Halibut—Broiled or Boiled

A slice of halibut, owing to the bone structure and its placement, is very easily divided lengthwise and crosswise to the central small bone; with a small slice this will give four portions, with a larger one, each of these sections may again be halved, now following the grain or flake of the fish.

Note to Madame: Because of its small percentage of bone, halibut, despite its slightly greater cost per pound, is actually one of the most economical fish to buy.

Whole Boiled Salmon

This beautiful sea food—"King of Fishes"—known to have existed thousands of years before the birth of Christ, is often served whole. Elaborately garnished with cool lemon and cucumber slices and fennel or parsley, it is indeed a royal dish.

"Whole" means that both head and tail are left in place and incidentally the salmon may be either hot or cold, though due to its richness, it is especially delicious cold.

Place on the platter, head to the left. To serve, cut carefully through the skin at the central (back) bone, then carve down as far as the bone into slices about one inch wide, cutting from back to belly, then slipping the knife under the flesh to separate it from the backbone. Serve a little of the thick solid back meat and the thinner more fatty flank to each guest. Lift out the bone and proceed in exactly the same manner with the under side of the fish.

Where a cut of salmon, say one to three pounds, is boiled and served, the carving will be done in exactly the same manner. As with most fish the center cuts are the choicest, but many, men particularly, like the head with its rather glutinous, though small amount, of flesh.

Broiled Salmon

For this service being "steaked" before broiling no carving is necessary unless the steaks are very large in which case divide evenly right through the center at one side of the bone.

Boiled Cod

Any cut, head and shoulders, center cut, or tail, is usually served smothered in a sauce. Carve exactly as boiled salmon, but remember that as the flakes of the cod are large and loose, it is a more difficult fish to serve attractively.

"Garnishes—the ornamentation that set it (food) forth just as a lady wears her jewels to give piquancy to her natural charms."

Theodore Garrett

Garnishes and Accompaniments

WHILE this is in no sense a cook book it seems not amiss to say just a word here regarding garnishes and meat accompaniments. The proof of the pudding probably is in the eating but a lot depends on the sauce too. Artistry and imagination play a large part in the service of food and a deft touch often works wonders in making even good food more interesting. This added touch need not entail very much labor or expense, but it must be there or our meals will become monotonous to the cook and fail to intrigue the interest of the diners.

The importance of skillful garnishing of food is rarely sufficiently emphasized. This though must not be taken to mean that garnishes should be over elaborate. Moreover it ought to go without saying that they themselves should be edible

—indeed someone has gone so far as to define the term "garnish" as "one food used to decorate another."

Color too is important but not too much of it for a little goes a long way. Such easily obtainable inexpensive colorful garnishes as green and red peppers, pimientoes, very small red and yellow tomatoes, radishes, olives (plain, stuffed or ripe), lemons, hard-cooked eggs, watercress and parsley to name but a few of the most ordinary, add immeasurably to the decorative scheme of one's table.

Use contrasts in color, generally speaking garnishing light bland foods with dark rich garnishes and contrariwise the heavier foods with delicate tones and flavors.

Don't be afraid to be original, provided you keep your originality within reasonable bounds.

Don't garnish everything that is served at a meal—there should always be one high spot of color and of flavor.

And what about accompaniments to our meats? Some things naturally belong, some don't. French fried potatoes with corned beef for example would be anathema, so would sauerkraut with turkey. Each of these is good in its place, but let's keep them in that place.

We can't tell you exactly what to do at all times but we can at least give you a few ideas of "what goes well with what."

What to Serve with Meat

BEEF

	Garnish, Sauce or Relish	Accompaniments Starchy	Green
Roast Beef	Scraped Fresh Horseradish English Mustard	Yorkshire Pudding Franconia or Baked Potatoes	Spinach, Corn, Brussels Sprouts, Green Beans Stuffed Peppers or Tomatoes
Steak	Mushrooms—Broiled Sautéed or Stuffed French Fried Onion Rings Grilled Tomatoes Maitre d'Hôtel or Horse-radish Butter Brown, Mushroom or Bear-naise Sauce Watermelon Pickles	Duchesse, Lattice, French Fried, Shoestring, Lyon-naise or Pimiento Potatoes	Green Peas, Lima Beans, Sliced To-matoes, Broccoli, Creamed or Fried Onions

[114]

	Garnish, Sauce or Relish	Accompaniments Starchy	Accompaniments Green
Pot Roast	Brown Sauce or Gravy (A few cranberries or dried apricots cooked with the roast)	Potato Dumplings or Pancakes Plain Boiled Potatoes Noodles or Spaghetti	Carrots Turnips Onions Celery
Corned Beef	Mustard Mustard Pickles	Boiled Potatoes	Cabbage Beets Onions Carrots Turnips
Tongue, Hot	Horseradish, Raisin or Cider Sauce	Parsley or Creamed Potatoes	Spinach Squash Lima Beans Carrots Escalloped Tomatoes

VEAL

	Garnish, Sauce or Relish	*Starchy*	*Green*
		Accompaniments	
Roast Veal	Mushroom or Fruit Stuffing	Browned Potatoes	Broccoli
	Brown or Mushroom Sauce	Mashed Sweet	Green Beans
	Currant or Grape Jelly	Potatoes	Peas
			Cole Slaw
Veal Cutlet or Chops	Tomato or Brown Sauce	Mashed or Riced Potatoes	Stewed Tomatoes
	Olives	Potato Croquettes	Asparagus tips
	Currant or Cranberry Jelly	Macaroni or Spaghetti	Peas
			Mashed Parsnips

LAMB

Roast Lamb	Mint Sauce or Jelly	Parsley Potato Balls	Green Peas
	Currant Mint Jelly	Minted New Potatoes	Asparagus
	Bar le Duc		Creamed Onions
	White Turnip or Beet Cups filled with Peas or Young Lima Beans		

	Garnish, Sauce or Relish	Starchy	Accompaniments	Green
Boiled Lamb	Onion or Caper Sauce	Plain Boiled Potatoes	Carrots	Turnips
				Braised Celery
Lamb Chops	Sautéed Pineapple Slices	Parsley Potatoes	Green beans	
	Glacé Orange Slices	Creamed Potatoes	Corn-on-Cob	
	Baked Bananas		Peas	
	Currant Jelly			

PORK

	Garnish, Sauce or Relish	Starchy	Accompaniments	Green
Roast Pork	Celery, Sage and Onion or	Mashed or Baked	Brussels Sprouts	
	Apple and Raisin Stuffing	Sweet Potatoes	Braised Celery	
	Apple, Cider or Cranberry		Onions	
	Sauce		Baked Squash	
			Sauerkraut	
Pork Chops	Apple Jelly or Butter	Boiled or Grilled	Stewed Tomatoes	
	Chili Sauce	Sweet Potatoes	Mashed Turnips	
	Broiled Bananas	Noodles	Red Cabbage	
	Grilled Pineapple Slices or			
	Apple Rings			
	Raisin-Stuffed Apples			

[117]

	Garnish, Sauce or Relish	Accompaniments Starchy	Green
Fresh Spareribs	Stuffed Apples Cranberry Relish Onion Rings	Baked Potatoes Escalloped Potatoes	Mashed Turnips Cole Slaw
Baked Ham	Apple Rings Apples—Plain Baked or Raisin-Stuffed Raisin Sauce or Currant Jelly Sauce Cranberry or Cider Sauce Grilled Bananas or Pineapple Slices Mustard	Mashed Potatoes Glacé Sweet Potatoes	Any preferred green vegetable

COLD MEATS

	Garnish, Sauce or Relish	Accompaniments Starchy	Green
Beef Veal Lamb Pork Ham	Mustard or Horseradish Grape Conserve Mint or Currant Jelly Apple Sauce Cranberry or Apple Jelly	Potato Salad or Mixed Vegetable Salad or	Cole Slaw or Mixed Tossed Green Salad preferably with French Dressing or a variation of French Dressing

POULTRY AND GAME

	Garnish, Sauce or Relish	Starchy	Green
		Accompaniments	
Roast Turkey	Bread, Oyster, Sausage, or Chestnut Stuffing Spiced Pears or Peaches (Stuffed with India Relish) Crisp Little Sausages Cranberry Jelly, Sauce or Sherbet	Mashed Potatoes Browned Potatoes Glacé Sweet Potatoes	Peas Green Beans Corn Creamed Onions Turnips
Roast Chicken or Capon	Bread, Chestnut, Celery or Oyster Stuffing Spiced Fruit—Crabapples, Pears, Peaches or Kumquats Cranberry Jelly or Sauce Currant Jelly Baked Orange Halves Sautéed Pineapple Fingers Crisp Little Sausages	Mashed Potatoes Browned Potatoes Glacé Sweet Potatoes Steamed Rice	Corn Peas Asparagus Tips Green Beans

	Accompaniments		
	Garnish, Sauce or Relish	*Starchy*	*Green*
Roast Duck or Goose	Sage and Onion, Celery or Apple and Raisin Stuffing Orange Sauce or Sherbet Apple Sauce or Stuffed Apples Cranberry Jelly Currant Jelly Sauce	Wild Rice Rice Croquettes	Peas Turnips Braised Celery
Wild Duck	Savory Stuffing Lemon Butter Baked Orange Slices or Halves Currant Jelly	Hominy Cakes	Tossed Green Salad
Rabbit or Hare	Forcemeat Balls Currant Jelly Grape Jelly	Sweet Potatoes	Corn-Stuffed Tomatoes or Peppers
Game Birds: Pheasant Partridge Quail, etc.	Bread Sauce Buttered Crumbs Cut Lemon Currant, Grape or Wild Plum Jelly	Rice or Potato Croquettes	

[120]

FISH

Because fish is apt to be less popular than meat it is highly essential to make it attractive and interesting in appearance. A few garnishes and accompaniments sometimes overlooked are:

Lemon or lime slices, cut attractively, sometimes sprinkled or edged with finely minced parsley.

Halved lemon cups filled with Maitre d'Hôtel, Hollandaise or Tartare Sauce.

Watercress, chicory.

Anchovy butter balls, lemon butter balls.

Asparagus tips (in bundles held together by green pepper or pimiento rings).

Cold beet cups filled with diced dressed cucumber.

Hot beet cups filled with peas or tiny lima beans.

What to Serve with Fish

		Accompaniments	
	Sauce or Garnish	Starchy	Green
Boiled Fish	Oyster, Lobster, Egg, Mustard, Parsley or Shrimp Sauce Lemon	Parsley or Pimiento Potatoes	Spinach Peas Green Beans Beets
Broiled or Fried Fish	Maitre d'Hôtel or Brown Butter Tartare Sauce Sliced Cucumber Lemon	French Fried, Shoe-string, Oven-Frenched, Hashed Brown or Stuffed Potatoes	Peas, Carrots, Broccoli, Eggplant Sliced Tomatoes Stuffed Tomatoes or Peppers
Baked Fish	Shrimp, Bread or Celery Stuffing Lemon	Baked, Escalloped or Au Gratin Potatoes	Stewed Tomatoes Wax Beans Cauliflower Cole Slaw

Index

INDEX

INDEX

INDEX

INDEX

[127]

9446